Trever's Biscuit

L.D. Pegram Boyle

AuthorHouse™
1663 Liberty Drive
Bloomington, IN 47403
www.authorhouse.com
Phone: 833-262-8899

Because of the dynamic nature of the Internet, any web addresses or links contained in this book may have changed
since publication and may no longer be valid. The views expressed in this work are solely those of the author and do not
necessarily reflect the views of the publisher, and the publisher hereby disclaims any responsibility for them.

Any people depicted in stock imagery provided by Getty Images are models,
and such images are being used for illustrative purposes only.
Certain stock imagery © Getty Images.

This book is printed on acid-free paper.

ISBN: 978-1-4490-8266-6 (sc)
ISBN: 978-1-5049-0259-5 (hc)

Print information available on the last page.

Published by AuthorHouse 09/29/2023

authorHOUSE®

Acknowledgments

I would like to thank the following people:

David and Sue Resenbeck, owners of Hoosier Kennels. Without their photos of their dog Bell and her puppies, this would not have been possible.

Carolyn Winkler, with her skills, who did all my beautiful illustrations.

Dr. Ralph Welp, veterinarian, and his assistant, Bonnie Pinkston.

Barbara Litschgi, a friend and inspiration.

On a blustery, snowy day, Bell had her new puppies, and one of those puppies will soon be named Biscuit!

This is Bell's first litter of puppies.

Five girls and three boys are born. It looks like one of the puppies might be hiding in a corner!

The cute, little puppies are black and tan furry balls. They are all safe inside the big box with their mother, Bell.

Trever, just like most six-year-old boys, is very excited about getting his new puppy. Trever likes the puppy that always hides. He decides to name her Biscuit because she looks like the color of a biscuit.

The puppies love to cuddle together and lie on top of each other.

Biscuit is taking a little nap and dreaming about cuddling with the black puppy.

Every day, the puppies grow bigger and stronger. Now they are big enough to start eating Puppy Chow.

Soon Biscuit will leave her first home and go to Trever's house.

Trever is waiting for Biscuit to grow bigger so she can be strong enough to leave her mother Bell. Trever needs to start getting ready for Biscuit to come to his house.

Biscuit needs a safe place when she comes to Trever's home. She will also need a food bowl, a water bowl, some toys, a new collar with a leash, and a soft bed to cuddle in.

Trever is so excited because Biscuit is going home with him today.

It looks like Biscuit is ready to go with Trever!

Biscuit is sad the first night in her new home because she is missing her mother, Bell, and her brothers and sisters. Biscuit cries and howls all night long.

Trever cuddles with Biscuit and tells her a story of how all her brothers and sisters will have new homes with other loving families.

The next day, Biscuit forgets all about the sad night. Biscuit is happy just running around and playing with her toys.

Biscuit and Trever are having lots of fun playing together!
Biscuit really likes her new home and Trever's family.

Biscuit is growing bigger and bigger and can run faster than Trever now. Biscuit is so happy playing with her toys. She makes all kinds of funny noises!

Sometimes Biscuit wants to go outside to her big house and sit in the sunshine. Biscuit has lots of room to run and play.

It is safe for Biscuit to go outside. She even has a big shade tree to keep her cool.

When Biscuit goes outside, she likes to watch Trever's grand-pa working in the garden. Biscuit is waiting for a carrot to eat!

Biscuit is peeking between the fence rails, still waiting for Trever's grandpa to give her a carrot.

Sometimes Biscuit gets into trouble. She sees a rabbit while she's waiting for Trever's grandpa to give her a carrot. The little rabbit is busy hopping around and eating lettuce and does not see Biscuit.

Biscuit takes off running after the rabbit! The rabbit runs very fast and gets away from Biscuit.

The rabbit finds a hiding place in a hole, and Biscuit gets lost in the woods behind the garden for a short time.

Biscuit finds her way back home. For Trever, it seemed like Biscuit was gone for a long time! Trever is so glad that Biscuit is home now. Biscuit has forgotten all about the carrot.

Biscuit has had a big day outside, playing in the yard and chasing the rabbit. She likes to take a nap on her back on the floor after playing.

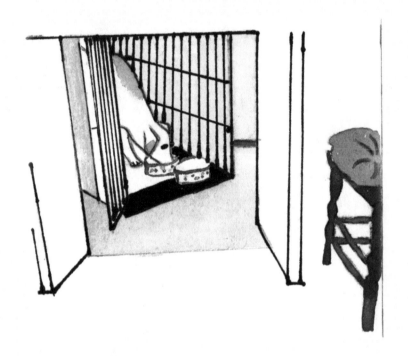

After napping and having so much exercise, Biscuit is very hungry and ready to eat her Puppy Chow.

Biscuit is always happy at the end of the day, after playing outside.

After a full night's rest, Biscuit wants out of her little house.
She nudges the door with her nose to open it.

Every day, Biscuit needs lots of care from Trever and his family. Biscuit needs fresh water every day.

Biscuit likes to drink lots of water. She has two bowls of fresh water to drink from. Her favorite water bowl is the blue bowl. That was Biscuit's first water bowl when she was a puppy.

Every year, Trever needs to take Biscuit to the doggie doctor.
She needs to have a good checkup.

Trever does not want Biscuit to get sick.

Biscuit likes to go to the doggie doctor. She gets to see the nice people who work there, and she gets a treat too! Biscuit has her leash on and is ready to go!

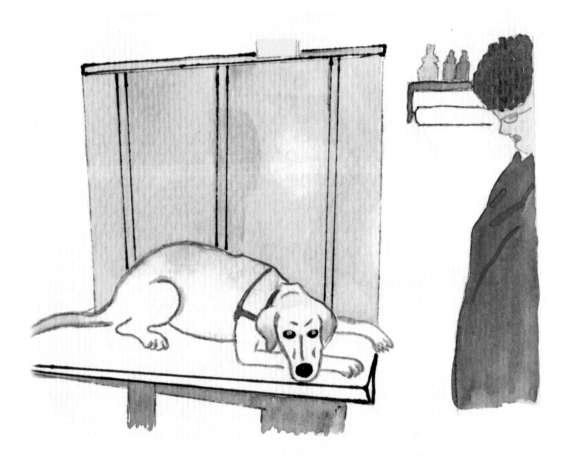

The doggie doctor will weigh Biscuit to see how much she has grown. The doggie doctor will also look at her teeth and check her ears.

Biscuit gets a good doctor's report. Now the doctor is ready to send Biscuit home.

Biscuit is ready for her car ride back home. She pokes her head out the window and sniffs the air.

Biscuit is so happy to be back home. She can run and play with her buddy ball and Trever.

She likes to play football with Trever, too. Biscuit always wants
to keep the fun football.

Biscuit and Trever are even happier together now! She loves her new home.

Biscuit and Trever will be friends forever. Biscuit has many, many fun days ahead!

Notes from Biscuit

I have grown up to be a big girl.

I go out every day for play and exercise.

I always have fun watching Trever's grandpa working in the garden and yard.

Last summer, Trever's grandma took me to visit my first home at the Hoosier Kennels.

That was a lot of fun for me because my mother, Bell, and my sister Rosie were there.

Trever's grandma entered me in the 2008 Pet Calendar Contest. She told me about winning fourth place. There was a picture of me and Trever in the newspaper and on the calendar month of December—my birth month!

2009

Taylee with her buddy Biscuit

Printed in the United States
by Baker & Taylor Publisher Services